This Morning

BOOKS BY MICHAEL RYAN

POETRY

This Morning

New and Selected Poems

God Hunger

In Winter

Threats Instead of Trees

PROSE

Baby B

A Difficult Grace

Secret Life

This Morning

POEMS

MICHAEL RYAN

HOUGHTON MIFFLIN HARCOURT
Boston   New York   2012

811.54
Ryan

For information about permission to reproduce selections from this book, write to Permissions, Houghton Mifflin Harcourt Publishing Company, 215 Park Avenue South, New York, New York 10003.

www.hmhbooks.com

Library of Congress Cataloging-in-Publication Data
Ryan, Michael, date.
This morning : poems / Michael Ryan.
p. cm.
ISBN 978-0-547-68459-8
I. Title.
PS3568.Y39T45 2012
811'.54 – dc23
2011042370

Book design by Greta D. Sibley

Printed in the United States of America
DOC 10 9 8 7 6 5 4 3 2 1

For Doreen and Emily

CONTENTS

III

I

SIXTIETH-BIRTHDAY DINNER

If in the men's room of our favorite restaurant
while blissfully pissing *riserva spumante*
I punch the wall because I am so old,
I promise not to punch too carelessly.

Our friend Franco cooks all night and day
to transform blood and bones to osso buco.
He shouldn't have to clean them off his wall
or worry that a customer gone cuckoo

has mushed his knuckles like a slugger
whose steroid dosage needs a little tweaking.
My life with you has been beyond beyond
and there's nothing beyond it I'm seeking.

I just don't want to leave it, and I am
with every silken bite of tiramisu.
I wouldn't mind being dead
if I could still be with you.

A CARTOON OF HURT

Burglar noise brought me downstairs bare-chested
wielding my daughter's aluminum softball bat
as if in three A.M. living-room shadowland
I'd be terrible Hector instead of a senior English professor

and there you were, my father —
forty years dead, rummaging my liquor,
younger than me now and ageless and faint,
your grip too soft to lift the fifths and quarts

but rattling them to the old family music:
falsetto amber-bottle-scrape-and-clink of a man
rushing to fix himself a drink, as you always did
the moment you came home from work.

How could you be so unchanged by death?
Even out of this world you want out of this world.
— Unchanged in me, I guess. Watching you,
aluminum softball bat drooping like a penis,

I'm a cartoon of hurt, embarrassed by it.
"Dad," I whimper, but you can't hear it.
You abandon the liquor to open the refrigerator.
Its sudden light flashes through you like a bomb blast.

The twist-off beer caps shred your hands to Kleenex.
The pulltab of a tallboy pulls half a finger off.
You howl in pain you couldn't feel but felt,
the same pain of yours I couldn't feel but felt,

which now morphs obligingly into all my ugliness,
demons and ogres dancing in my kitchen,
envy and resentment, despair and disappointment
spitting and farting, sticking out their thorned tongues.

AIRPLANE FOOD

Compressed chicken product, festive succotashed rice,
dead iceberg lettuce with a pale cherry tomato
hard as a mothball, and the coup de grâce: a baby bundt cake
I expect will taste like my passport
but to my delight is not bad,
half bad, or even sort of bad: it is good.
Good good good good good all good
this plain sweet baby bundt cake like much else
I shall never taste touch hear see or smell,
baked for the heavens in its own fluted tube pan
for every blessed one of us ticketed passengers,
purely for our pleasure and then only briefly –
ingested, enjoyed, absorbed, and fading from memory
since we lack the capacity to retaste baby bundt cake
unlike the many childhood wounds I experience
half a century later from the faintest reminders.
This same baby bundt cake might seem scandalous
to the incognito *Michelin Guide* reviewer
in a three-star restaurant in the south of France.
It could cost the owner-and-chef all his stars
when losing one drives such men to relentless self-torment.
It could cause his wife-the-hostess to cease loving him
instantly, if she had worked eighty-hour weeks with him in concert
painstakingly perfecting the desserts they were known for.
"Marcel, have you lost your senses?"
she'd scream (in French, of course).

"This bundt cake tastes like Michael Ryan's passport!"
All right, she wouldn't say like my passport
but some local invective for culinary blasphemy
such as "this bundt cake tastes like duck drop –
the underside of a sink – reduction of pig bristle –
your incontinent mother's bidet brush holder" –
an untranslatable invective for premeditated betrayals
like secretly developing and serving a recipe
based on the winner of a Pillsbury Bake-Off.
God knows what happened after their disgrace
to the couple, or their employees, much less their children,
especially the boy who loved nothing more
than working in the kitchen alongside his parents.
He certainly wouldn't touch a bundt cake for the rest of his life.
The sight of someone enjoying one could make him furious
and the aroma of baking bundt cake wafting from a Paris apartment,
unidentifiable to other strollers among the aromas of the city,
could make him weep as automatically as turning a faucet.
He would never discuss the bundt cake episode in interviews
after he had revolutionized the national pastry
and become famous for his supernal puffy napoleons.
Bundt cake could mean only his father's sudden dementia
and the years of grief and poverty suffered by his family,
but, since my experience and circumstances are so different,
I thought this bundt cake was really good.

DACHAU

Dachau isn't *Dachau*
to the people who live there:
it's like "Chapel Hill" or "Charlottesville"
only smaller and older, the quaint
medieval city preserved meticulously
at its center, innocent and neat,
as if to say, "Here's history too"
to tourists like me who come for the death camp.
This is what's disturbing about it:
the citizens of Dachau aren't wrong
not to not have children anymore
and slowly starve themselves to death
on an eight-hundred-calorie diet,
or even – though this is less certain –
not to drop to their knees every morning
and press their foreheads to the ground
and weep for what they allowed to happen.
The most hopeful idea of all – that no matter what,
life goes on – in Dachau
becomes horrifying. People buying toothpaste,
lunching on delicious beer and *Weisswurst* –
as if nothing's heinous enough
to permanently eradicate commerce and good cheer,
love and friendship and laughter
that express how unfathomably lucky it is
just to be alive. But isn't this terrifying?

It means humans can do anything
to one another and go on living.

Dachau could be an advertisement for it,
such pastel charm and calm and beauty
while the death camp squats on the outskirts:
aptly closed the day I took the train from Munich –
aptly to its place in my life
born into postwar prosperity in the United States
as skeletons stumbled out of death camps
I didn't see even on newsreels until I was in college.
Their specter, the specter of being a good German
as I read now about tortures in Iraq and Guantánamo,
which are no doubt a fraction of what's hidden,
made me feel I'd better see what I can in person.
The cab driver, a bright retired woman
who was only a baby during the war,
drove me through kilometer after kilometer
of manicured farmland, and when I mentioned
how far from town the Nazis built the death camp,
she said the townspeople then
never spoke of it, they knew but didn't want to know
what was going on out there, and this common agreement
was so effective that some people
actually were surprised when they "found out"
after the war was over.

Was this the story she told to tourists?
Then it was there: a low fortress,
eerily unimposing, startlingly small,
a few acres defined by an eight-foot concrete wall
topped with double struts of barbed wire,
nothing like a maximum security prison now
at Guantánamo or anywhere else.
I did a chin-up to hold my face above the concrete
and peer through the strands of barbed wire
and, though I didn't expect rusty gasworks
and blood-soaked mud, the fresh white
clapboard cottages and trimmed lawns criss-crossed
with gravel paths looked like a prep school campus
or, at worst, an army base, shut down.
I held myself up as long as I could
to feel my weight hurt the soft flesh of my hands
before I let myself down. "It's pretty bizarre,"
I said more to myself than to the cab driver
as I slid onto the back seat's padded leather
and cupped its soothing plumpness in my palms.
She turned and smiled as if at a child
and asked, "It's a pretty bazaar?"

(June 2005)

I HAD A TAPEWORM

I had a tapeworm, and imagined it
flat – paper-flat – like a strip of caps,
pallid red, a quarter-inch wide
with bulbous BB bullfrog eyes
peeking out of my asshole as I lolled
in a crowded fetid basement swimming pool
(the kind that used to be in inner-city Y's:
windowless; steamy; concrete-block moldings
chalky-cracked), and you whom I've neither
seen nor heard of for thirty years
were saying I'd give everyone in the pool
my tapeworm, which you knew had eaten
my insides and now had threaded through
both my intestines and was trying to get out.
Where were we? Everyone was old, old –
gray, infirm; flaccid and thin
or fat and bald, all ill flesh drooping –
the women in rubber-flowered bathing caps
and black one-piece suits as if we were all
on an outing from a nursing home.
I couldn't see myself to see how old I was,
but you were thirty, at the peak of your beauty,
as when you knelt naked on the motel room bed
brushing out your thick dark waist-length hair
after cheating on the lover you were cheating
on your husband with, who was at that moment

11

waiting for you in another motel room
from which you had slipped to meet me secretly:
a secret inside a secret, buried, encased,
as if if we dug deep enough into it
we'd find what we were trying
to get or stop.

FUCKED UP

I needed to be wanted
So I made myself into
Someone you would look at
If he looked at you.

You were cute (or not) and smart (or not),
A lovely soul (or not) –
What mattered most to me about you
Was if I made you hot.

You think I didn't know even then
What this meant about me?
I was not the only one
Locked in fantasy

Because real life was terrifying
And difficult and dull.
Which made you (plural squared)
Irreplaceable.

Of all enslavements, not the worst.
But there weren't enough of you,
And many too many others
Who so easily saw through

The ecstatic adventure I offered
To my self-loathing despair
That the creep with the come-on look
Simply was not there.

He's still not there, or anywhere.
It's years since he's been fed.
But he likes to bite my brain
To show me he's not dead

And means to own my life again
And flip it north to south,
All my sweetest thoughts of you
Dripping from his mouth.

HALF MILE DOWN

My sick heart and my sick soul
I'd gladly fasten in a bag
and drop into an ocean hole
to float in darkness as a rag.

Would it learn to make its light?
Maybe in a million years.
A million years of constant night
in which it can't stop its fears

flaring their nightmare tentacles
and bioluminescent eyes
as cold and sharp as icicles
under moonless, starless skies:

medusae, spookfish, cephalopods,
jellies with no eyes or brains,
lethal and beautiful as gods,
locked in endless predation chains.

How seamless then the world would seem,
which life on earth never did,
the living water like a dream
crowded with prowling vampire squid

that want only to stay alive
among other monsters innocent
of all but the pure drive to survive
without self-judgment.

INSULT

Before you went out I asked you
in no uncertain terms to button
the next button up your shirt
that showed your naked breast
from the right angle when you twisted
and bent, an angle admittedly rarely
reproduced in real-world space
and then what would need to be in place
is the mythical irresistible male
whose lust could flare furiously
(like mine) and push you ecstatically
beyond where you sexually go
with me. Obviously I don't know
what would be possible for you
with a body other than mine,
but I love you and yours so dearly
the thought's too much for me
despite your saying your love for me
makes the idea preposterous
from the get-go. I'm sorry
I spoke harshly. My jealousy
is a jealous companion.
It wants me alone.

NO WARNING NO REASON

Because he left her, she must make him
someone she doesn't love, rescripting as
deception their hand-clasped walks at dusk
when she felt his was the hand of God
linking her to him because she was
so blessed to be given this love
this late in life. It must have been lies:
each touching word, all thoughtfulness,
his shows of pleasure putting her first,
his endearing sex talk that first
amused her then got to her
(his hot moist breath the poison in her ear)
as he learned with seemingly selfless patience
how to move inside her as no one ever had before.
How can she change memories like these?
He must have been lying
because the man who did these things
could not leave her with no warning or reason.
But she knows he wasn't,
and, because she knows he wasn't,
she is stuck. No one can help her.
No one can enter the sacred circle they made together
she now wears as a necklace of fire.
How can she obliterate the person he is?
What is she to do? She has to live.

HARD TIMES

The lousy job my father lands
I'm tickled pink to celebrate.
My mother's rosary-pinching hands
stack pigs in blankets on a plate.

Teeny uncircumcised Buddha penises
(cocktail hot dogs in strips of dough):
I gobble these puffed-up weenie geniuses
as if they'd tell me what I need to know

to get the fuck out of here.
They don't only stink of fear.
They're doom and shame and dumb pig fate.
I tell my mom I think they're great.

Dad chews his slowly with a pint of gin,
and says he eats a whole shit deal
because of us. My mom's in tears again.
I don't know who to hate or how to feel.

MY YOUNG MOTHER

What she couldn't give me
she gave me those long nights
she sat up with me feverish
and sweating in my sleep
when I had no idea whatsoever
what she had to do to suffer
the pain her body dealt her
to assuage the pain in mine.

That was a noble privacy —
her mothering as a practice of patience.
How deeply it must have stretched her
to watch me all night with her nerves
crying for rest while my fever
spiked under the washcloths
she passed between my forehead
and her dishpan filled with ice.

That was a noble privacy.
But even then there was so much
unsayable between us,
and why this was now looks so
ludicrous in its old costume of shame
that I wish not that she had just
said it but that I hadn't been
so furious she couldn't.

ODD MOMENT

Live your values said a voice
that wasn't a voice at all,
although I heard it on the phone
when I picked up the phone to call

my mother, who died
six months ago.
What was I thinking of?
I know

she's dead. I touched her hands
(a knuckle, really – and very lightly)
as she lay in the silk-lined box.
I absolutely

couldn't kiss her sunken face goodbye
as others were able to.
After I knelt near her a while,
there was nothing else to do

because she needed nothing from me.
How can a life just be *done?*
Done also what life was to her
alone, which no one

else can comprehend,
even (or especially) her son.
Is this why I forgot she's dead
and picked up the phone

to punch in her number
believing she'd answer,
and my brain said what she'd say
to me? Is she not done with me?

IN THE MIRROR

The death I see
coming to me
stops to chat
more frequently.

"How's my good man?"
he asks, all grin
and bonhomie.
He can get in

any body-hole.
I squeeze mine shut,
don't even breathe.
He can hear what

I think, so I don't,
except for *Go.*
Because he's fast,
I try to be slow —

slow as prehistory,
slow as a stone,
slow as eternity,
slow as alone.

"I *am* Alone,"
he boasts. "It's fun.
I get to kiss
everyone."

His lips become
a luscious bed.
"A kiss from me
and you'd drop dead.

"I'm the last one
you will see.
If I were you,
I'd be nicer to me."

What in the world
would *that* mean?
I'm afraid to ask.
Something obscene

no doubt he looks
red hot to say.
Is it possible
death is gay?

"Of course I am —
or, rather, bi.
How do you think
women die?"

He heard my thought —
I forgot he can.
"Why would you want
to be a man?"

I finally ask aloud.
"You *are* thick,"
he replies. "If you were
a brick I'd be a brick.

"I'm the mirror
of your sorry soul.
I reflect you
completely whole."

And when I look
I can see
him melting back
into me:

his lips, his eyes,
his razor brains.
My doughy wrinkles.
My spider veins.

THE DOG

The neighbors' baby died age one month
so they're off to Big Sur "to celebrate her life"
and I stupidly agreed to feed their dog –
a twelve-year-old wire-haired mix, half-blind,
half-dead itself, its gum lines receded to a rictus grin.
What was I supposed to say when the husband asked?
"Your baby's dead, but I can't be bothered.
I don't really know you. Ask someone else.
I don't like your dog. I think it's hideous.
What if *it* dies while you're away?
I'm supposed to call and tell you that?
I don't want to touch it.
What if your misfortune is contagious?"
But I said, "Be glad to," and he embraced me,
this Kurt or Kirk, I'm not even sure which.
"Siobhan" – that's his wife – "can't stand to kennel her,"
he sobbed into my shoulder, his eye rims moistening
behind his clownish owlish oversized glasses
he knocked askew against my clavicle.
It startled me so much I couldn't guess
who "her" referred to until I got he meant the dog.
All *her*'s: the dead baby, the wife, and now the dog.

I *don't* like the dog. It stinks. It needs a bath.
Who washes a dog during a month like that?
But I'll be damned if I'm going to do it –

dried dogshit or worse matted in hair
the color and texture of rusted wire
caked with rotted moldy drywall.
The dog howls all day – and I mean *all* day –
as if these were the feelings left inside the house.
From outside all month the house had been silent
except the one time early on the paramedics came
so the neighborhood knew a disaster was happening.
I never doubted for a moment there was wailing inside,
including the baby's, which must have been constant.
But the dog didn't howl until everyone was gone.

Siobhan has to be forty-something –
They supposedly did a doula water birth at home,
her husband assisting, no doctor, no amnio,
no genetic testing – I think they belong
to some megachurch where the pastor
the size of a fish stick from the bleacher seats
projects fifty feet high with his bleached teeth
and they sing-along upbeat Christian music
ten thousand strong, as loudly as they can.
"To celebrate her life": the pastor's phrase, I bet.
If that helps them bear it, fine.
All I know is I have their dog to deal with.
One thing I'm not doing besides wash it
is walk it, so I called a franchised service

that sent a Belarusian with a crescent nose stud
(God knows what *his* story is)
who rang my doorbell after half an hour.
"I can't walk dog," he said. "It won't go.
It won't leave house. I think it sick.
You better take it to vet." So I did.
Again I picked one from the phonebook,
who charged me eighty bucks to find a loose tooth,
although he offered a thousand dollars' worth of tests.
"The dog is old," he said. Oh. Thanks.
Then I tried at home pretending the dog was mine,
actually petting it (a bit) and talking in goofy baby tones
while giving liver chips and Buddy Biscuits and playing fetch,
but, while I napped, it scratched off the front-door paint
and started gnawing its way out.
After I gated it back in the neighbors' kitchen
with its blanket and bowls and dried bull pizzle,
it began howling again, which is what it's doing now.

Maybe there's something in the house still.
Maybe tiny syringes and bandages upstairs
the dog smells. It would be too odd to go up there
where the baby was, into the baby's room,
with the neighbors' hopes there as furniture,
pink bunny or smiley angel or kiddie Bible wallpaper.
It would be like being inside their privacy,

their intimacy, their monthlong nightmare.
Maybe I have to call them after all.
I hate to call them – they should have peace
to grieve enough to live again in a house
that no matter what they believe or understand
will never be for one moment as they thought.
I don't know what else to do but call them.
Their dog – their ugly old dog – is howling for them
and will not stop.

MUG

Glaze crazed and lip chipped, my beloved mug
has suffered one too many Hi-Temp Power Scrubs
that unglue from my pots their antediluvian pot-crud
but must have felt like burning hurricanes
to my pint-size off-white faux-porcelain darling.
How could I have blithely slept
while she was being buffeted on the top rack
amid thick glass tumblers and impervious Tupperware?
How could I be so blind to put her
through this recurring Armageddon nightmare
when all she needed was a warm hand-wash
and cool air-dry upside-down on a dishtowel?
Delicate, in truth, she wasn't. MADE IN CHINA
tattooed on her bottom, she was always cheap
and probably dangerous: her black underlayer
now showing through the crazed glaze like varicose veins
no doubt leached into my blood the thousand times
I filled her to the utmost with dark roast
and took her hot lip between my lips.
At such moments, who thinks what's underneath:
lead or cadmium or reprocessed industrial waste?
Mornings before the house was awake,
in exquisite quiet and not-yet-light,
I'd cup her tenderly in both hands,
breathing her heat, not needing to speak.
I felt so happily posthumous,

just this side of nothingness, alone but not.
I didn't need to be anything for her
but an eager mouth – not a nice husband
or good son or even a man – only the unregenerate
consumer that I am. I savored every dram.
Everything later was decaf,
dull paper cups in mousy brown sleeves
served by contractually cheery Starbucks drones
amid chatter and laptops and cell phones.
But I knew tomorrow morning she'd be sparkling,
ready to give back whatever I put in,
and we'd have our time together again,
respite with no pretense of nourishment,
her first bitter droplet on my tongue tip.
How sad that it may have been toxic.
I'd bury her in the backyard like a pet,
except she could pollute the aquifer.
Goodbye, beloved mug. No recrimination. No regret.
(At least until my next blood test.)
I had not one unpleasant moment with you.
Who in the world can anyone say that about?
I'd like to think I somehow gave you pleasure too.
Maybe we'll meet again in another life,
me the mug next time, you the mouth.

GARBAGE TRUCK

Once I had two strong young men hanging off my butt
and a distinctive stink that announced
when I was inching down your street
at the regal, elephantine pace
that let my men step down from me running
to heave your garbage into my gut
then fling the clanging metal cans
to tumble and rumble, crash and leap
back to sort-of-where you'd lugged them to the curb
before another oblivious night of sleep.
Did you think life was tough?
I reveled in it, all the stuff
you threw out, used up, let rot,
the pretty packaging, the scum, the snot,
vomit and filth, everything you thought
useless, dangerous, or repugnant:
I ate it for breakfast. I hauled it
out of sight. And what did I get?
You were annoyed by my noise.
You coughed at my exhaust.
Your kids stopped playing in the street
to pinch their noses and gag theatrically
with no clue how sick they'd be without me.
I was the lowest of the low, an untouchable,
yet I did what I did and did it well.

Now I am not laughable: a "waste management vehicle"
denatured robotic sanitized presentable.
My strong young men are gone. I have no smell.
I'm painted deep green to look organic and clean.
Your "residential trash carts" are matching green
injection-molded high-density polyethylene
that barely thuds when I lower them to the ground
after I've stabbed and lifted and upended them
with twin prongs that retract into my side
so not to scratch anything or scare anyone.
Who can complain? Right there on your street
I mash and compact and obliterate your waste.
You need never give it a second thought.
It's safe it's easy nobody gets dirty.
It's how you want your life to be.
But life's not garbage. Garbage is life.
Look what you've got. Look what you throw out.

THE DAILY NEWS

I needed to be made to feel that there was real,
permanent happiness in tranquil contemplation.
Wordsworth taught me this, not only without
turning away from, but with a greatly increased
interest in the common feelings and common
destiny of human beings.
          — J. S. Mill

Out walking in my nature-or-nurture,
culture-or-creature, we-are-all-fucked
funk, I wandered like great-browed Wordsworth
lonely as a cloud upon his daffodils,
ruined abbeys, and sagacious peasant workers
eager to engage in earnest dialogue with
and spark a personal-but-socially-useful meditation for
a happening-to-be-strolling-by major British poet

and happened myself upon
a wackily painted California-beach-town clunker
with a strikingly somber
NEVER FORGET GOD white-on-black bumper sticker
precisely centered on its back bumper.
I thought, "That's straight out of Flannery O'Connor,"
only she'd have the car hurtling through,
packed with a family masterfully
tormenting one another,

          or loaded with murderers
on their way to a murder, or idling
while its owner (an itinerant preacher –
half Christ, half con man, all heartbreaker)
performs some grace-provoking mischief
on a spinster. I don't know who
owns this car and I certainly don't want to know,
but were he a guest on Wordsworth's call-in show,

I'd ask him from anonymous distance, "Never forget God?
How do you do that? My faith comes and goes.
I can't even speak about it without distortion.
Never forget: is that the same as always remember?
Who remembers anything always?" At that point,
he'd probably answer, "Just a minute,"
and, switching the control dial back to Flannery O'Connor,
he'd reach into the glove compartment
for the gleaming, silver, startlingly high-tech
automatic pistol and the pack of evangelical pamphlets
from which he slips one with a rubber-band snap
that makes me jump as if he'd clicked the gun,
a pamphlet that on my walk home I would curl into
a little glossy telescope, focus on a flower,
and toss into the next garbage can

after this unwordsworthy contemplation of nature
reminded me to retune and retune
and retune my attention,

which the car had already done,
                it being
adorned, as I have not yet said, with multicolor
lightning bolts, asterisks, question marks,
and squiggles, a '74 Dodge Dart Swinger (I think)

that no doubt in previous incarnations
served emotionally less expressive owners
ferrying children to soccer practice and doctors
and all the-world-is-too-much-with-us getting-and-spending
required of us to earn moments of private life and quiet pleasure
(its dead shocks perhaps once cushioning
the hurried rhythms of backseat lovers) –

whose paint job (whatever muted colors it had been then)
now features a purple trunk-spanning skull and crossbones
above the NEVER FORGET GOD bumper sticker,
and one modestly trussed mermaid in red-polka-dot halter
reclining along the entire length of the passenger side
from rear to front fender, with what little space
left in the negative space around her

maniacally scratched in with tiny druidic glyphs,
which, could we read them, would rebuke us
for our idolatrous, splintered common life.

SPLITSVILLE

If you get yours I get mine.
How does never sound to you?
As long as I can laugh I'm fine.
I can't believe this all is true.

If I were gone you'd be all right.
What is that supposed to mean?
I see you're looking for a fight.
You are such the drama queen.

Let's get the hell out of here.
I'm simply not leaving yet.
Everything you say is fear.
Maybe you ought to buy a pet.

What do you want if I'm not it?
If you don't shut up, I will scream.
I feel like such a piece of shit.
I thought you were a living dream.

MELANOMA CLINIC INFUSION CENTER
WAITING AREA

This ravaged man, this human specimen:
extra-high black nylon windbreaker collar
zipped up, extra-wide soft floppy hat brim
yanked down – to spare beginners here his creature

face and spare him being seen:
eyebrowless and -lashless, chemical-
burned inside-out and outside-in:
irradiated, interferoned, Dacarbazined, his skull

a scar he looks out from through the Gitmo slit
between upturned collar and downturned hat brim
at the doings of what must seem another planet
than the one he's on inside his body killing him.

How he bears it he's not telling. Not telling
may be part of the how. Maybe he's been given
access now to such unencumbered clarity of feeling
it makes what can be spoken sound like pidgin,

and so he rests in articulate silence,
communing like Buddha with his own spirit.
But probably not. Probably the malignance
eating his being, minute by minute,

has beaten him into its mute instrument
of pain and loneliness and fear.
There may be sweet freedom in the firmament.
Not here.

OPEN WINDOW TRUCK NOISE 3 A.M.

Gear-grinding, sure, but the woman dreaming in 4F
sees the monster spawned by her boss's daily belittlements
devour in one roaring gulp both the Smith Barney courier
in the apartment across the air shaft who comes home from work and strips
to the black Brazilian thong he likes to parade around in
and his insomniac schnauzer that yaps at fire-escape cats.
What monster is this? There's no name for it,
nor for the rancor that forms it
nightly inside her brain, and it *is* merely a chimera
safely encased in thick skull bone,
but on the morning she spies the suddenly kimono-clad courier
feeding his schnauzer a croissant, she remembers
what woke her was her boss drilling her skull a borehole
for the monster to fly out like a cockroach
that owns her and walks her to work on a leash.

DAREDEVIL

Although he's only seven, you can pick him out
from other first-graders: he's the one wearing
a smirk that says, "What are you afraid of?"
maybe also to himself, if he already suspects his fear
won't ever be crushed no matter what he does.
But he's got to try. He snatches spiders bare-fingered
to wave in girls' faces, bites a worm in half
dangling the two ends from his mouth like fangs,
somersault-dismounts from the jungle gym
the other kids climb off of when he climbs on,
and when he lands unhurt there's that smirk again
that mocks us for our cowardice.
Don't hate him for it. It is his only happiness.

HERE I AM

on a subway station bench
next to two teens, one pretty, one not:
the pretty one keeps saying how much
she'll miss the unpretty one, kissing her cheeks,
while the unpretty one looks down at her lap
saying no you won't no you won't until the train comes
and on goes the pretty one still smiling,
twirling her red plastic clutch, singing goodbye
I'll call you, and the unpretty one just sits here
like a stone, even after the train is gone,
even after I write this down.

SABBATICAL

I'm full of feelings, all of them boring,
so today I let my poem take me
where it wants to go, as if the *where*
were a patio overlooking Lake Como
where Bellagio Fellows discuss the quattrocento
over a rare Barolo and my poem
were a complimentary airport minivan
driven by a spiky Iraqi
bursting with bitterness that pops
his English inflections like an M-16
which for all I know he wore over his shoulder
day after day in sucking desert heat and fitted
with a nightscope and slammed the butt of
into whatever wasn't moving fast enough.

A ROUND

Where am I going? The grave.
Who am I being? The slave.
What am I leaving? The fun.
Who will be grieving? No one.

How can I touch you? No way.
Will I ever reach you? Someday.
Why do I need you? Ho ho.
Where will I meet you? You know.

FUNERAL

"Hi, sweetie. Coming home,"
were the last words she left
on your cell phone,
so now, bereft,

you blast them
through rock-concert speakers
as if to annihilate all thought
except of her.

"How about that shit?"
you ask us in the service,
while we get more and more nervous
you'll collapse

right here and now
forever
during your furious
eulogy of her.

"Hit by a fucking bread truck!
Can you *believe* it?"
you shout at us. Yes, we can.
No, we cannot.

Husband your grief now,
since you must.
It won't leave you.
Don't leave us.

for PML

ILL WIND

Two red birds
high on a wire
one said love
one said fire

Two black birds
deep in a tree
one said you
one said me

But wind came up
and tossed them away
no one hears
what they say

AGAINST WHICH

habit smacks
its dull skull
like a stuck bull
in a brick stall

and my version
of what I know
is like eye surgery
with a backhoe

on grace
so much beyond
my pitiful gray
sponge of a brain

I'd not believe it exists
except for such
doses of felicity
as this.

VERY HOT DAY

I know what's going to happen
to those two plastic produce bags of crushed ice
I perched atop the garden wall:
one's floppy, droopy, flabby,
its overhanging pooch of ice-melt
already about to pull the whole bag down
into the dirt, bursting it, turning it
into a fistful of filthy gummy polyethylene;
the other's centered, poised – even
its ice-melt seems to know where to settle
so the bag stays upright and stable:
if it were a person, he'd radiate
smiling confidence and good health,
a team player wanting only to be useful,
to stand as an example of how to adjust
conflicting parts of himself for the general good.
His effortless balance and bright red twisty-tie
might seem flashy and arrogant
were he not so persistently mindful
that he shares the other bag's fate.
How could he not, since they're almost touching?
He'd have to be completely oblivious
not to witness the moment his twin
plops into the dirt.
He'd have to know he's heading there too,
no matter how solid he feels at present –

that even now he's really broken and helpless
and destined for the recycle bin
where like Almighty God I throw
useless used bags for crushed ice
the butcher gives me to keep my raw meat
safe while I drive home on a very hot day.

SUSTENANCE

Having awakened again at 4 A.M. inside the skull-dungeon
in which my brain's chained like a nasty old man
grumbling, blustering, keeping me from sleeping,
I focused as suggested on my breathing,
asked blessings on every living human being
alphabetically, one at a time,
except for a certain book reviewer,
all poohbahs owning eight or more Porsches,
most politicians, patricians, and registered Republicans,
gave up, got up, and was being lowered gently
into quiescence by reading good writing
when *slambangclang* a garbage can
behind the screened window behind my reading chair
upended. Yogis spend lifetimes
emptying mundane consciousness enough
that the body, as if it had been weighted
by thought, might levitate a quarter-inch,
but I shot six feet to the ceiling in a nanosecond,
still seated, hovering like a tenth-ton hummingbird
until nasty old brain-man informed me dryly
what was outside wasn't human.
I killed my reading lamp and shone a flashlight
through the window: a cartoon raccoon
in cartoon burglar mask dissecting
my actual plastic trash bags with her
dexterous, delicate, spidery claws.

Tell me this animal is not intelligent.
She had climbed onto the garbage can
and rocked it to knock it down.
About me and my flashlight beam
she was utterly incurious.
I wish I were so fearless.
For five minutes of our respective lives
I got to watch her eat some chicken bones
(I thought I cleaned pretty well myself
three days ago), flipping them
like batons to gnaw the ungnawed ends:
neither a strung-out meth head with a handgun
nor revelation engendering enduring peace of mind
but an earthly privilege, gratis,
despite the holy mess she left for me
I'm glad was food.

EARPHONES

Autumn in our kitchen, hooked up
to a Discman (Bach's Sonatas and Partitas for Solo Violin),
I become the music with earphones on:
no noise-as-usual inside my skull,
I can do things so the doing seems to be coming
from not-me, I am so expert and prolific
at rutabaga soup, peeling and chopping with such prowess,
spicing with panache, fussily tasting and adjusting,
even cleaning the pot and utensils, wiping the counter,
the sink, the cutting board – so happy, my darling,
that I despite myself have made something good for you
you will never have to suffer or work for.
Look, it's waiting in your favorite blue bowl
with fresh bread and wine beside it.
Come, sit, my loveliness, my blessing:
Come, sit, and eat it with me.

PETTING ZOO

I should be able to learn something useful
watching 20 toddlers in a 12   12 pen with 20 animals.
But they're alien creatures – the kids, not the animals.
The animals are Zen masters: dispassionate, imperturbable,
despite whompings from long-handled curry brushes
distributed by merry adolescent lime-shirted attendants
then wielded as cudgels by the darling torturers.
The sixty-five-pound tortoise especially is getting it.
Three consummate cuties drum *Bolero* on his shell.
The tortoise is seventeen according to the parents' info sheet
so he's in for two hundred more years of this.
I also identify with the shampooed pin-curled potbelly pig
sporting a saddle on which is strapped a stuffed bunny
whose sewn-on smile riding above the mayhem
is as maniacal as a crusader's charging into battle.
The actual bunnies, by contrast, all would go AWOL:
they escape one toddler only to be scooped up by another –
also a metaphor for parenting (but a useful one?),
including parenting an only child like mine.
My darling torturer is a fierce creature. She pets me
precisely when she pleases, but it inevitably fills me
with immeasurable sweetness. Talk about addicted to love:
at her birth, my well-being vaulted out of my body
and lodged itself in hers. I'd much rather die than she die.
If these bunnies turned to vipers, I'd dive in to save her.
This makes me a garden-variety parent.

All we garden-variety parents elbow-to-elbow around the pen
have read that petting zoos swarm with *E. coli* bacteria
and have noted the baffling stack of unwrapped cookies
grinning innocently from a shelf bolted on the pen's gate
alongside the antibacterial-wipe dispenser.
My daughter methodically zigzags through the other toddlers
to cuddle every single animal. The ones too heavy to lift
she pats on the head, including the tortoise, whose skull
extends from his shell because it's less noisy, if more risky.
She has mashed ants and snails and watched transfixed while I killed
what she called a bitey spider but apparently hasn't applied
their mortality to herself and so radiates the confidence of a god.
Every thing in the world is here for her to play with and be delighted by.
Every place in the world welcomes her wholeheartedly, including this one.
After she has cuddled or petted every animal exactly twice,
she wants to spend quality time with her favorite:
a newborn chick that does not want to spend quality time with her.
Each time she unpries it from the belly fur of an angora rabbit
it thinks is its mother, it dives out of her hands as from a burning building.
So she settles for her second choice, the potbelly pig,
and unseats the stuffed bunny with a gladiatorial swat
and tries to mount the saddle, repeatedly and fortunately
unsuccessfully (quick pig) until I lure her out the pen's gate
by dangling before her nose a big infectious cookie.
As she grabs for it, I snatch her hand and wipe it thoroughly,
then her other hand, then every square millimeter of exposed flesh

up to her armpits – any place that could have touched an animal
or a kid who touched an animal – while she howls like Achilles
dipped into the River Styx. I frisbee the cookie into a trash can,
but buy her a popsicle, which stops her howling
as if she had never been disappointed and never would be again,
not so much forgiving me as entirely forgetting
as she takes my hand with her unoccupied one
for us to go into her next-moment adventure
hand in hand, for now locked together forever.

CAMPUS VAGRANT

"I no longer privilege myself," he says,
then makes his hand into a blade,
a chest-high single half a prayer
with my dollar he didn't ask for
slotted between his thumb and forefinger
as if in the cockpit of a rocket
that suddenly thrusts above his head
and snaps back to his chest, a blade again
he playfully jabs at me and folds into his pocket,
from which it emerges as his empty hand –
this sequence performed with practiced quickness.
"Did you stab me?" I ask. "Am I dead?"
"I stabbed you alive," he replies merrily,
his face lit up red as his Angels cap
with the halo at the apex of the A.
"Do you play for the Angels?" I once asked him.
"I play *with* the angels," he answered angrily,
and flicked my dollar crumpled back at me.
"Don't patronize me. I'm not crazy," he said.

I stick to our script strictly now,
although there's more I'd like to ask him.
I don't know how to "no longer privilege myself,"
if that means waking to egoless consciousness
in which fear and greed become so painless and harmless
I could float circles above them

like the halo on the logo.
My dollar vanishes into his pocket
and his hand always comes up empty,
but only after his ritual gesture
up to something other and higher
then down to himself to stab me alive
enough to love my life more
desperately as it disappears.

THIS MORNING

My daughter was crying before she went out to play
because the sunscreen on her face made her hair sticky
so when she tried to put on her glasses
that have rubber cables that loop behind her ears
she kept snagging her hair
and hurting herself. She cried, "My hair won't stay back"
so I said, "I can hold your hair"
and gathered it into my hands to cup behind her head
while she pulled on her glasses, and when I did
I felt beneath the unearthly lightness of her hair
the ridges of her skull. Her skull's a little asymmetrical –
we didn't lay her on her stomach as an infant
because she had neurosurgery when she was seven months old
for a birth defect, a tethered spinal cord, a minor spina bifida
she probably got because her parents were so old
she had to be conceived in vitro.
But who knows? She's almost eight now.
Why it happened doesn't matter to us anymore.
She must be checked neurologically every year.
The spinal cord can retether until she's fully grown
and fray essential nerves that allow her
to walk and control her bladder.
When we take her to the doctor's for her checkup,
there are kids in hockey helmets and wheelchairs
with their heads lolling and tongues hanging out,
drooling, bellowing, unable to speak with words.

I don't know how their parents do it –
probably because they have no other choice
but not-doing it, which they couldn't live with.
So they live with it, and I'm invariably surprised
to see them smile and joke and be patient,
which some are remarkably. They even understand
what their children are saying with grunts and groans.
They even make them laugh with tickling games
or goofy faces or hiding a rubber squeeze toy beneath their shirts.
They even laugh themselves,
and, because they do, our daughter does.
What she likes most is to laugh. You should see her laugh.
And her hair – you should see her hair – radiant light browns
over darker and darker underlayers that overflowed my hands this morning
while I held her hair for her.

CONTENTMENT

Fragile, provisional, it comes unbidden
as evening: the children on the block
called in to dinner that for tonight
is plentiful, as if it had cost nothing
either in money or worry about money.

Then evening deepens and the street
turns silent. There may be disasters
idling in driveways, and countless distresses
sharpening, but all that matters
most that must be done is done.

HAPPY ANNIVERSARY

The jolt that opened me to you
and shook me to my toes
needs no implanted seismograph
to read how deep it goes

because it's still rattling me
into this surprise
that the real dream begins
when I open my eyes

to see you so improbably here
and so entirely true
with all our random ducks lined up
for me to marry you

quacking a glorious Gloria
(transcribed into Duck)
to sexy earthy unnerving love
and astonishing good luck.

SPRING

Fat black bumblebees fucking in our yard –
orgiastic they knot up, five or six
like a buzzing fist looping in midair
until two lock and the lucky
couple snaps off and lands intact
hunching like puppies. They've even done it
on my armrest: the male's bent knees
clutched her hips for his teensy shudder.
Then he took off with no more ceremony
than if she had been a flower.
She seemed stunned, helpless
for all of a nanosecond.
You could almost see her shrug it off
before she too flew away, undamaged.

Is this more fun than the human version?
Come out again in your pink swimsuit,
my darling. The bees aren't swarming,
but I am.

MISS JOY

Husband dead, son grown and gone, her life
simplified – "her life" being a subject
almost independent of her and "simplified"
the verb through which her life acted
almost independently of her and what she wanted.
Her husband died suddenly and young
the week their son was born,
then there she was, bereaved and stunned,
trying to dig up money for a burial,
finding herself instead in a hole,
in deep grief, infant in arms,
inexorable in his needs as any infant is,
although her wishes for him were
all the stronger for her being alone –
her wishes being really only one wish:
that he have the chance to flourish.
Her vow to give him this she made
at the burial, but she made it
silently and only to herself.
Not until her son was grown and gone
did she see she had made it *for* herself
to give herself a reason to go on.
With this vow she made another –
never to give up sculpting –
which she thought then *was* for herself.
But she couldn't give her son the chance to flourish

unless she gave herself the chance in spirit,
and that meant sculpting whether or not
there would ever be any money from it.

And there hasn't been, except from teaching children
art classes in her bare-bones murphy-bed studio.
That's where I come in, way late and far
at the periphery, picking up my daughter Emily
age ten now who has been Miss Joy's student
since she was four. I rarely see Miss Joy.
Her classes were my wife Doreen's discovery.
When Doreen told me the teacher was "Miss Joy,"
I asked if Miss Joy had won a pageant
like Miss Galaxy or Miss Pork Belly
sponsored by a maker of antidepressants.
"Joy is her name," Doreen said, deadpan.
"Even the parents call her Miss Joy."
Today I know why:
she looks like a fresh birthday candle
with her tuft of white hair and soft bright smock,
and her eyes seem fired by what they see,
a delight in seeing she's taught Emily.
Miss Joy and Doreen have become friends.
Her story comes to me in pieces secondhand.

Have I made her seem saccharine?
I love her for loving Emily and Doreen.
I don't know what else she's done.
I don't hear much about her son
and even less of what she suffers.
Twisted metal scraps she finds in dumpsters
she hammers into battered solitary figures.

CONDOLENCE

The roses dying in your study
were never going to live forever.
The dancers study to embody
beauty: one is our daughter.

She exhausts herself. In thick leg warmers
she sprawls extravagantly on the couch
as if too sore to walk upstairs –
until she does, mouthing *ouchouchouch*.

She thrives inside our life together.
Where is it heading? How long will it last?
Hummingbirds keep returning to the feeder
we watch at breakfast through the glass.

How can we tell her what we see?
What can we give her now, or each other?
To what she loves she gives herself entirely.
We were never going to live forever.

GIRLS MIDDLE SCHOOL ORCHESTRA

They're all dressed up in carmine
floor-length velvet gowns, their upswirled hair
festooned with matching ribbons:
their fresh hopes and our fond hopes for them
infuse this sort-of-music as if happiness could actually be
each-plays-her-part-and-all-will-take-care-of-itself.
Their hearts unscarred under quartz lights
beam through the darkness in which we sit
to show us why we endured at home
the squeaking and squawking and botched notes
that now in concert are almost beautiful,
almost rendering this heartrending music
composed for an archduke who loved it so much
he spent his fortune for the musicians
who could bring it brilliantly to life.

ACKNOWLEDGMENTS

Thanks to the editors of the magazines in which these poems first appeared:

The American Poetry Review: "Condolence," "Contentment," "Dachau," "The Dog," "Fucked Up," "Funeral," "Garbage Truck," "Girls Middle School Orchestra," "Half Mile Down," "Happy Anniversary," "Here I Am," "Melanoma Infusion Center Waiting Area," "Miss Joy," "Odd Moment," "Open Window Truck Noise 3 A.M.," "Petting Zoo," "Splitsville," "Spring," "Sustenance," "This Morning," "Very Hot Day"

The Kenyon Review: "Campus Vagrant," "Daredevil," "Sabbatical"

The New Yorker: "A Cartoon of Hurt," "Earphones," "Ill Wind," "Insult," "No Warning No Reason," "Sixtieth-Birthday Dinner"

Poetry: "Against Which," "Hard Times," "I Had a Tapeworm"

Slate: "Mug," "My Young Mother"

The Threepenny Review: "Airplane Food," "In the Mirror"